D0100082

To My Father,
Whose affection
for Cats is
Legendary

Copyright © 1995 by Alan Snow. All rights reserved. No part of this book may be reproduced in any form or by any electronic or mechanical means, including information storage and retrieval systems, without permission in writing from the publisher, except by a reviewer who may quote brief passages in a review.

First U.S. Edition 1996. Published simultaneously in Great Britain by HarperCollins Publishers Ltd.

77-85 Fulham Palace Road, Hammersmith, London W6 8JB

ISBN 0-316-80282-4

Library of Congress Catalog Card Number 95-75414

10 9 8 7 6 5 4 3 2

Printed in Italy

The·Truth·About·Cats

·by·Alan·Snow·

Little, Brown and Company

Boston   New York   Toronto   London

Do you know where cats come from? Or what really lies beneath their soft and furry exterior? What do cats want from humans, and why are dogs their enemies? To discover the fascinating story of how cats came to live on Planet Earth, what the inner workings of these curious creatures look like, and why they have a secret mission, read on....

Contents

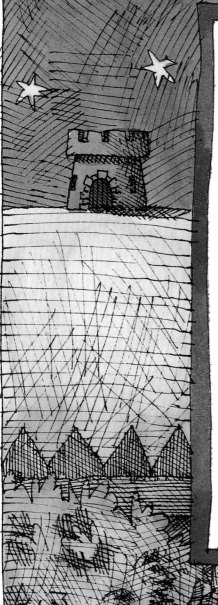

Capital city of the planet Nip →

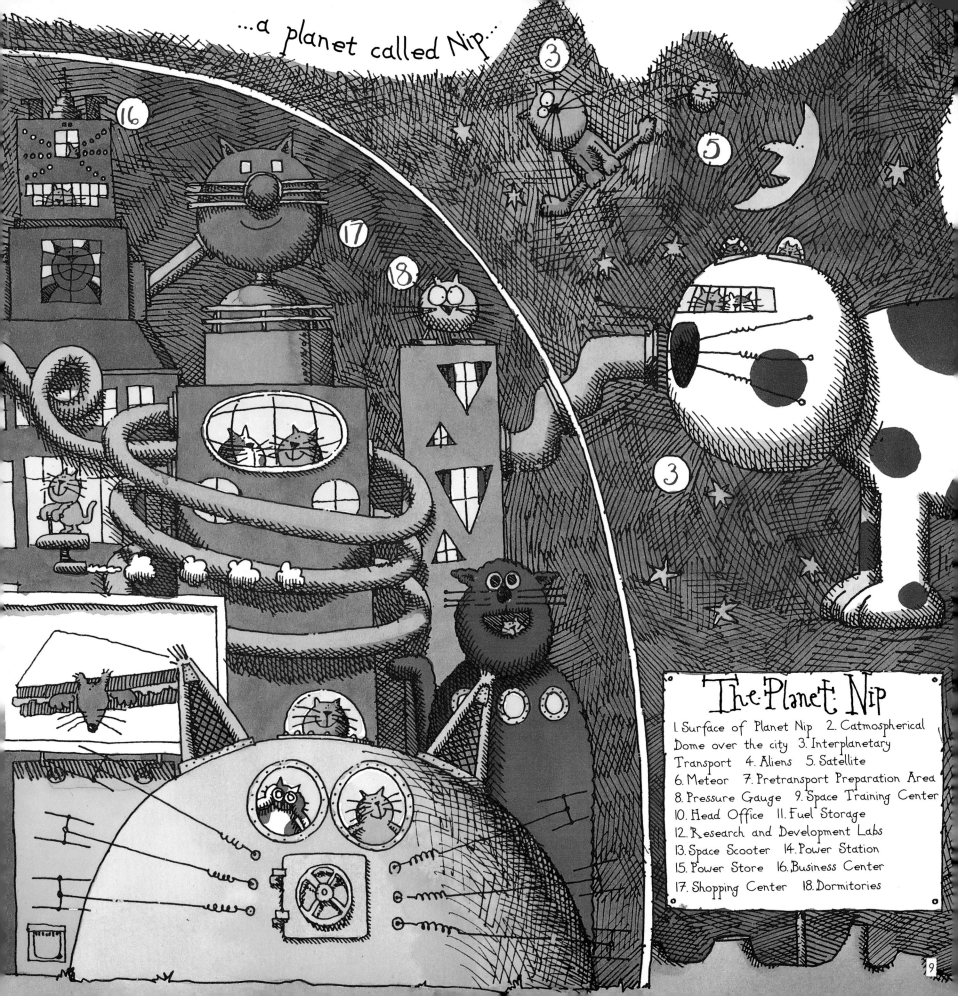

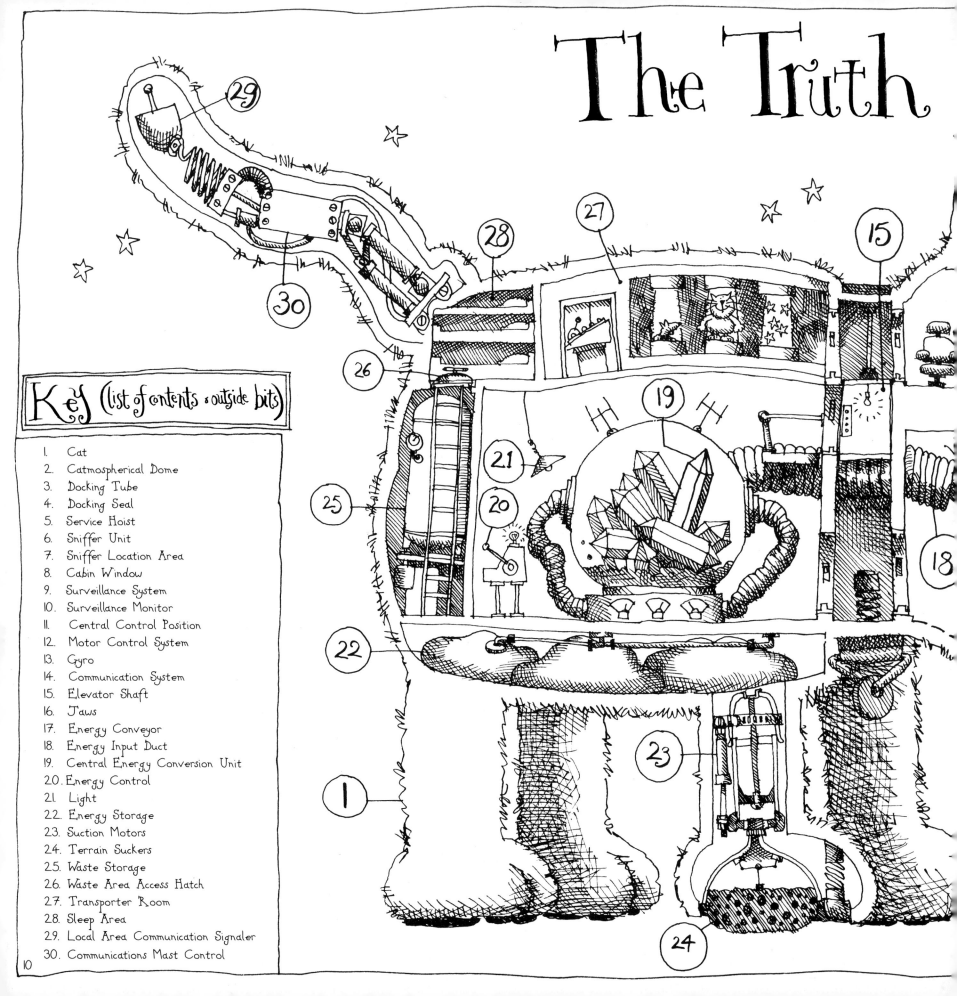

The Truth

About Cats

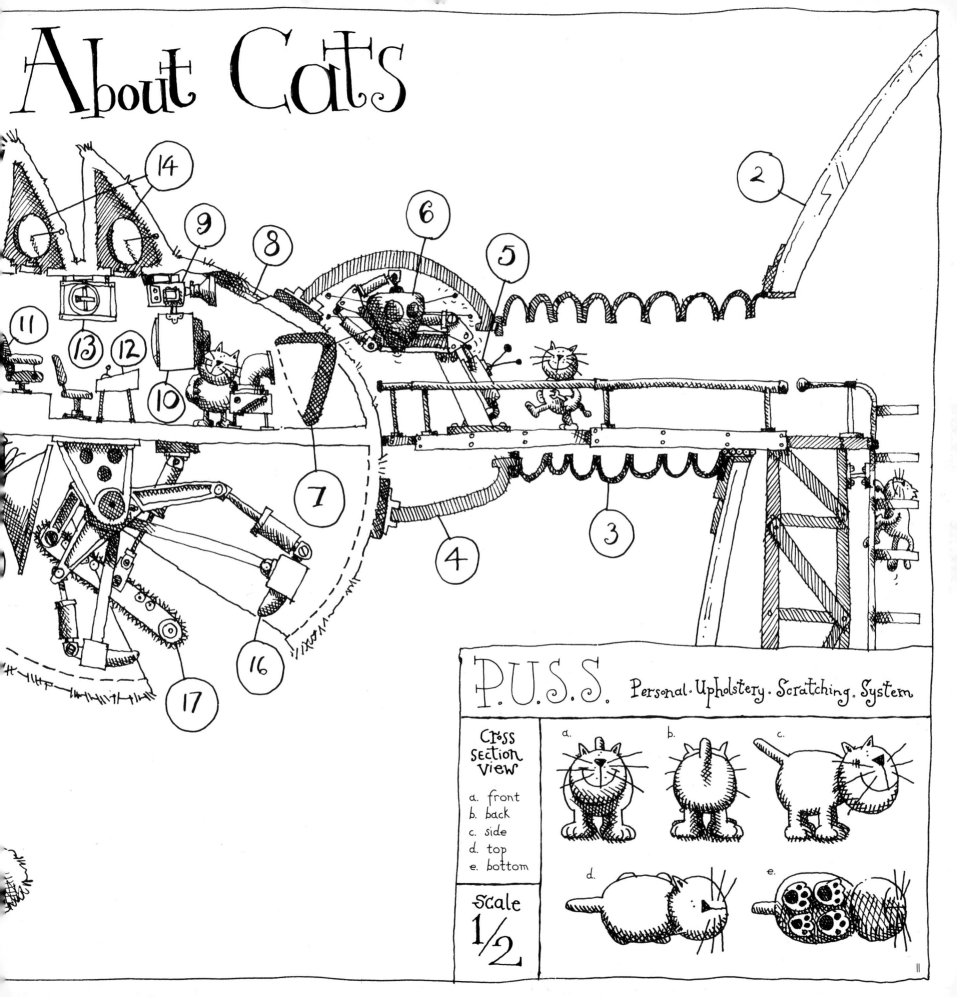

P.U.S.S. Personal·Upholstery·Scratching·System

Cross section view

a. front
b. back
c. side
d. top
e. bottom

Scale 1/2

Mission Earth ..!?!@☆

A long, long time ago, there were two races on Planet Nip: the Canines and the Felines. The Felines made life miserable for the Canines by jumping on their heads and forcing them to eat fish and lick themselves clean. The Canines got so tired of this that they built a primitive spaceship and set off to find a new home. After three weeks, they discovered Earth, where they made friends with humans and became known as dogs. They settled down to a happy and comfortable life until...

communication tuner

dog scanner

gyro system

elevator motor

communication headset

elevator

radar

memory system

washing machine

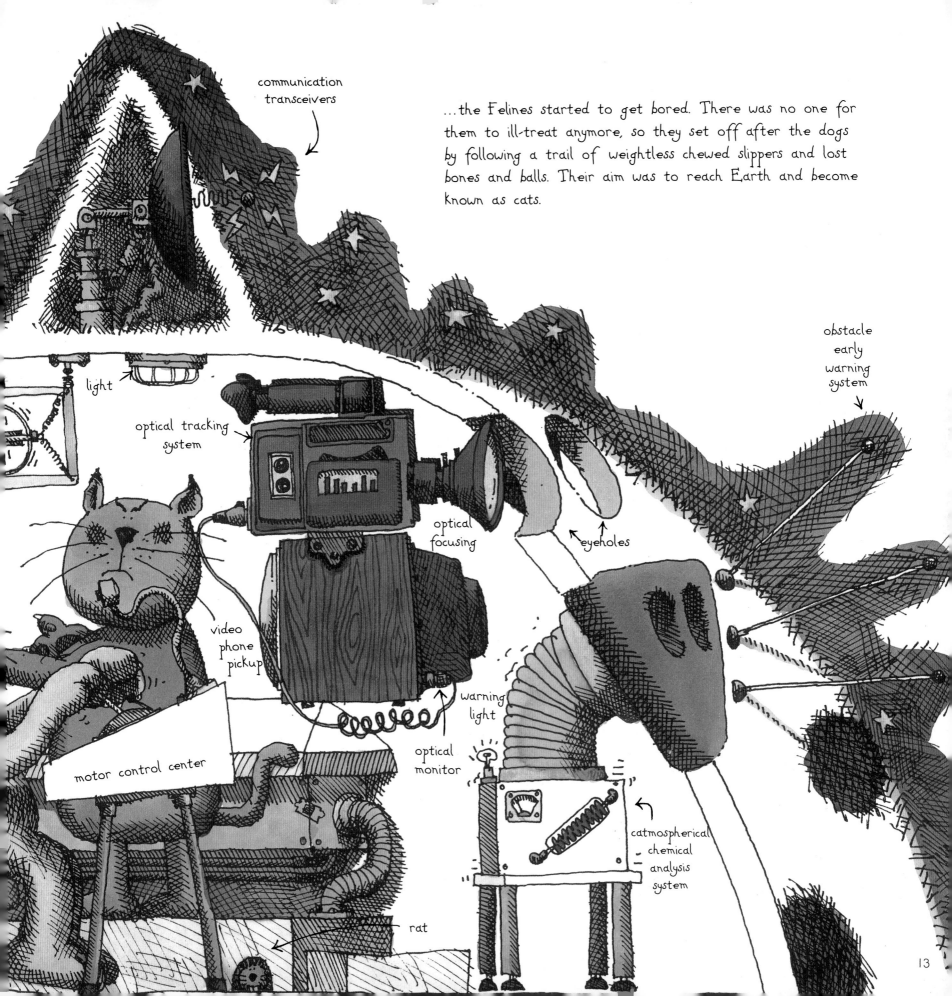

...the Felines started to get bored. There was no one for them to ill-treat anymore, so they set off after the dogs by following a trail of weightless chewed slippers and lost bones and balls. Their aim was to reach Earth and become known as cats.

communication transceivers

light

optical tracking system

optical focusing

eyeholes

obstacle early warning system

video phone pickup

motor control center

warning light

optical monitor

catmospherical chemical analysis system

rat

Space, The Final Frontier

And so the cats made their way through the fantastic vacuum that is space, across the mighty void, weaving between stars, asteroids, planets, and satellites, leaving behind the safety of home. The cats moved ever closer to the planet Earth, where the unsuspecting occupants were going about their business. Only the dogs on Earth had any idea what might happen.

15

Arrival on Earth

Cats usually arrive at night so as not to arouse suspicion. A cat who is already on the Earth's surface sends out a horrendously noisy signal to guide the orbiting cats toward Earth. As a rule, the cats aim to land on soft targets such as compost heaps, garbage dumps — and dogs! This can cause large quantities of dirt to become deeply embedded in the cat's outer shell, and it can take years for the cat to remove its last remnants. At any spare moment during its time on Earth, a cat can be seen trying to extract small particles of this debris from its upholstery with its paws or mouth.

Operating on Earth

positioning ram

Cats and Gravity

Cats have highly strung legs that are good for hanging on to things. They also have sensors to tell which way is up when they are falling. This allows cats to always fall on their feet (well, nearly always).

sensor movement

Once cats are on Earth, they use many complicated systems to get around.

monitor cameras

postcard   calendar

food store

cooker

communicator

sensor alert

cat on/off switch

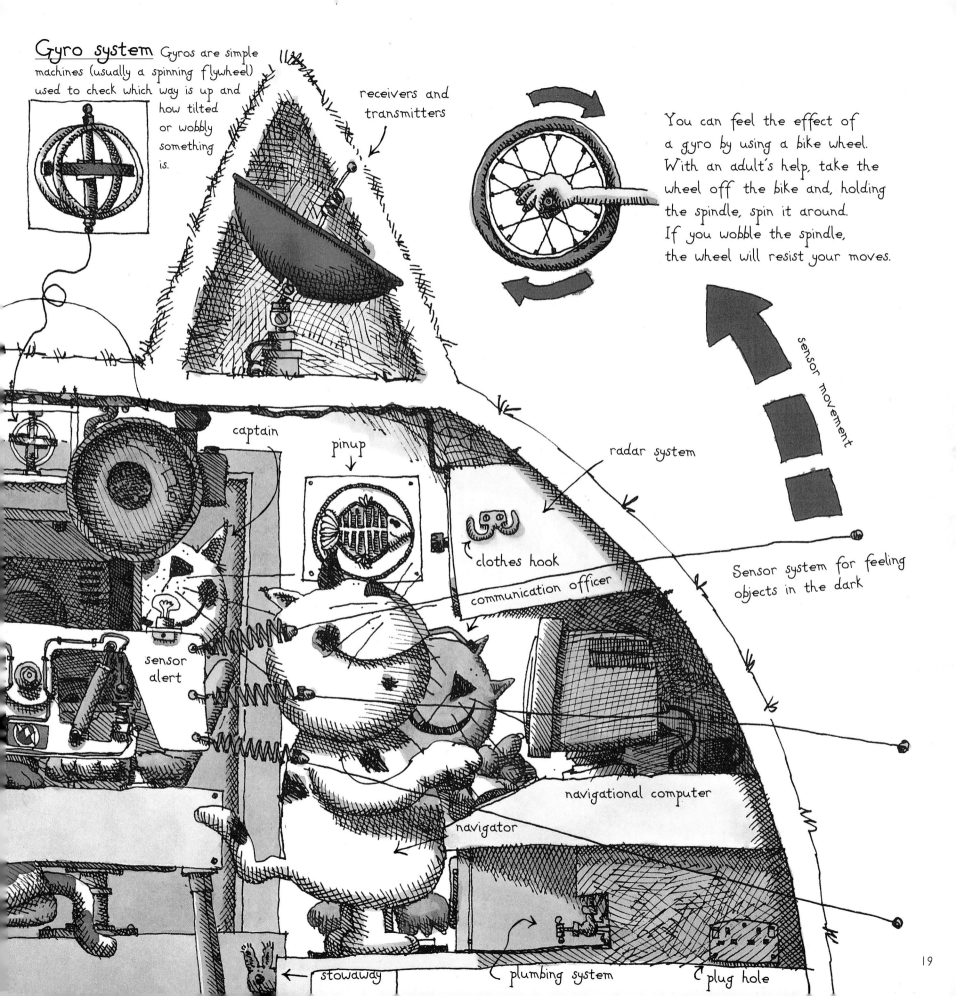

Gyro system Gyros are simple machines (usually a spinning flywheel) used to check which way is up and how tilted or wobbly something is.

receivers and transmitters

You can feel the effect of a gyro by using a bike wheel. With an adult's help, take the wheel off the bike and, holding the spindle, spin it around. If you wobble the spindle, the wheel will resist your moves.

sensor movement

captain

pinup

radar system

clothes hook

communication officer

Sensor system for feeling objects in the dark

sensor alert

navigational computer

navigator

stowaway

plumbing system

plug hole

Encounter...

As humans do not understand the danger, they often restrain the dogs until it is too late....

Dogs may try to communicate

but it is nearly always useless.

HELP SIGNALS (sent out to get help!) →

WARNING SIGNALS!!
Surface controlled to gain volume, giving illusion of greater size.

The secret and terrible mission of the cats is world domination and control of all fish supplies. Their first task is to drive out all dogs. This cannot be done just by confrontation, as dogs are usually bigger than cats. So cats must use tactics....

Tactic 1

Climb into tree using suction motors. Attract dog's attention. Wait until dog has exhausted itself barking. Drop on dog's head. Run away....

↑ dog odor

Crew of cats ready at battle stations.

Actions to be taken:
1. expand fur
2. point up ears
3. retract claw covers
4. calculate size of dog and chance of good outcome in conflict, calculate escape route (available trees, fence, etc.)
5. get legs ready
6. spit (yuck!) 7. run....

d Dogs (Part 1)

Tactic 2

Move in with family of dog-owning humans and gain their protection. Jump on dog or steal its food while humans are not looking. When dog reacts, wind your cat body around human legs. This will slowly but surely drive dog mad.

odor inlet

cat odor

Odor piped to dog brain causes brain to go to red alert status.

WARNING SIGNALS
Ears in warning position

Tactic 3

At night go to house where dog lives (when dog is locked in). Walk around yard or garden making high-pitched howling noises that only dogs can hear. Wait until dog has knocked him or herself insensible on the window trying to get you!!!

BARKING WARNING SIGNALS

Cats and Dogs (Part 2)

Inside the cat, at the heart of the control center...

Inside the cat control center, the dog is monitored on the visual monitor. The monitor system can be switched to very low light levels so the cat can operate even in darkness. The team, headed by the Captain, works out the best course of action....

monitor screen

dog

Don't worry... wait till he starts barking again, then full power, jump on his head and bounce over the gate!! He'll never suspect that!!

Captain
Duties include ordering equipment, reporting back to Planet Nip, and choosing lunch.

Captain, I've put up the deflector shields, but I think we have power for only another three minutes.

motor control center

Control of Humans

Humans are very easy for cats to control. Once power is gained over them, humans are useful for collecting food and providing protection. They can be trained to accept comings and goings at all times of day or night. This leaves cats free to pursue their master plan of world domination and control of all fish supplies.

Some humans can even be persuaded to build escape hatches into their own buildings, especially for cats. These should be just big enough for cats to squeeze through but just small enough for a dog's head to get stuck. Much fun can be had with these. Cats may appear too large for the hole, but this is just an illusion because they come from another planet space dimension!

Feeble-minded person being exposed to sympathy rays...

Watch out for the following signs in humans – any of these show that a cat is in control:
A weird desire to buy pretty cat collars.
Speaking in baby talk to adult cats.
Allowing cats to rip up and ruin expensive furniture.
Trekking around every shop in town to find just the right brand of cat food.

Enthusiastic glow (radiation from sympathy ray)

A large number of cats supported by a single human

Some humans are very feebleminded, and in these cases, total control can be gained with little effort. When this happens, a large number of cats can be supported by a single person, and their every whim will be catered for...fresh fish, transport, furniture for scratching, even total protection from dogs. Since the earliest of times, cats have been taking advantage of this, and throughout history they have wheedled their way into positions of power within many homes.

Even with the help of these feebleminded humans, cats have not yet succeeded in their mission. But, day by day, they gain more power. Their numbers are multiplying, and their hold over humans and dogs is strengthening. Dogs are already banned from many public places, while cats roam freely wherever they want. So be warned – complete cat control is not far away!

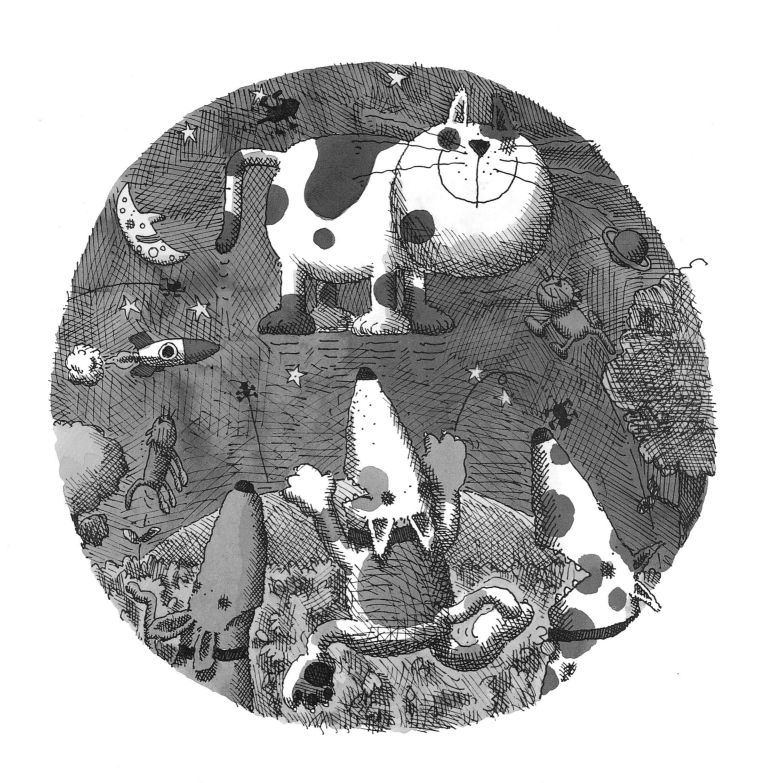

The End

Index